COLORS ALL AROUND

COLORES EN TODAS PARTES

Illustrated by Bo Young Kim • Ilustrado por Bo Young Kim

Lectura Books
Los Angeles

I see a Blue sky.
Veo un cielo Azul.

White clouds high in the sky.
Las nubes Blancas allá arriba en el cielo.

There is a Red ball.
Hay una pelota Roja.

A Yellow flower.
Una flor Amarilla.

The Brown earth.
La tierra Marrón.

And Green grass.
Y el césped Verde.

12

A Black cat on the grass.
Un gato Negro en el césped.

I see an Orange tree.

Veo un árbol Naranja.

And Purple plums on that tree.
Y ciruelas púrpuras en ese árbol.

Pink roses growing in the garden.

Rosas rosadas creciendo en el jardín.

I see colors all around.

Veo colores en todas partes.

23

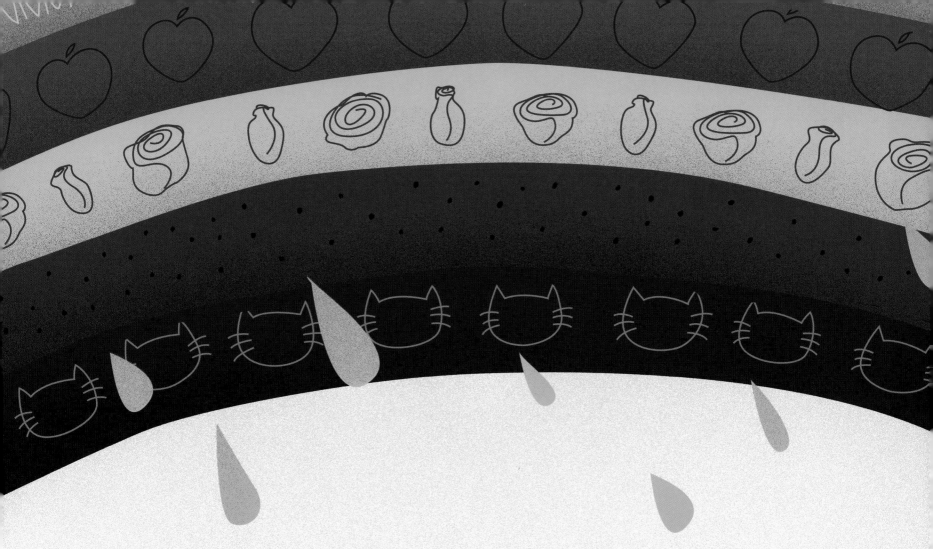

Like a Rainbow after the rain.
Como un Arco Iris después de la lluvia.

Blue
Azul

White
Blanco

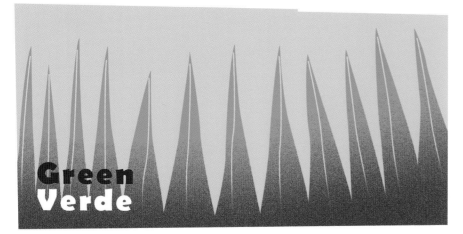

Green
Verde

Brown
Marrón

26

Yellow
Amarillo

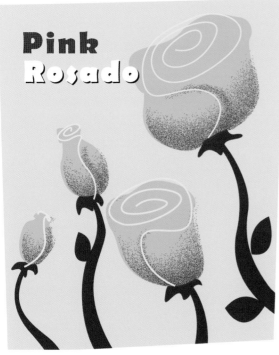

Pink
Rosado

Red
Rojo

Purple
Púrpura

Black
Negro

Rainbow
Arco Iris

Orange
Naranja

27

Copyright © 2009 Lectura Books

Publisher's Cataloging-In-Publication Data
(Prepared by The Donohue Group, Inc.)

Colors all around / illustrated by Bo Young Kim =
Colores en todas partes / ilustrado por Bo Young Kim.

    p. : ill. ; cm.

    Summary: Book presents basic color names in English and Spanish.

    ISBN: 978-1-60448-009-2 (soft cover)
    ISBN: 978-1-60448-013-9 (hard cover)

1. Colors--Juvenile literature. 2. Vocabulary.
3. Spanish language--Vocabulary.
4. Color. 5. Spanish language materials--Bilingual.
I. Kim, Bo Young. II. Title: Colores en todas partes

QC495.5 .C65 2008
752 [E]   2008937661

Lectura Books
1107 Fair Oaks Ave., Suite 225, South Pasadena, CA 91030
1-877-LECTURA • www.LecturaBooks.com

Printed in Singapore